GEORGE VILLIERS

POEMS

1919–1929

LONDON
THE HARVILL PRESS
1947

First published 1947
The Harvill Press Ltd.
23 Lower Belgrave Street, London S.W.1

Printed in Great Britain
at The Camelot Press, Southampton

Acknowledgements

SOME of these poems have appeared in the *Atlantic Monthly* and the *London Mercury*.

For permission to reprint them, our thanks are due to the Editors of these periodicals. Others were included in a small volume of verse which was privately printed in 1921. The rest are appearing for the first time.

Foreword

WHEN the First Great War broke out George Villiers had just left Oxford. So far he had written little, but the urge to write was there.

From 1914 to 1918 he served in the Grenadier Guards and was severely wounded in the Battle of Loos, receiving injuries from which he never entirely recovered and which, under the strain of service in a second war, were to cause his death in 1942.

In 1920 he produced a year's work in the form of a sixty-page book of verse which was privately printed. During the following decade his poems appeared in the *Atlantic Monthly*, the *London Mercury* and other similar periodicals. In 1932 the Oxford University Press published a collection of his verse. The poems appearing in the present collection come from the earlier period and some of them are taken from the book which was privately printed.

They belong intrinsically to the years which followed the end of the war and strikingly reflect the reactions of a personality which had come to manhood in a background of deep security and civilised values, to be fortuitously cast into the chaos, brutality and realism of battle. Throughout them is discernible the urgent desire to give voice to values which belong neither to the convention of the pre-war world nor to the expediency of a world at war; to reveal the sense of permanence inherent in the reiteration of the seasons, the repetitions of Nature and the unchanging life of the countryman; to recognise immutability in God. To find, as he wrote in another context, "The eternity of the past and the eternity of the future comprehended for a moment in the eternity of the present."

In this aspect the poems represent an escape from time, but this escape is always conditioned by desire to interpret, from the standpoint of the human spirit balanced between time and eternity, the joy and magnificence of Nature and the one-ness of humanity, a solidarity which, in his belief, remained unbroken vertically by the centuries, or horizontally by the clash of politics, race or creed.

Fourteen years later, in *Noonday and Nocturne*, he was again to give expression to these convictions. The mood and the form were very different, his own religious convictions had crystallised, but he re-interpreted the same values in the unpromising terms of the life of an overworked civil servant immured in a Ministry during the first six months of the Second Great War, and in this so different environ-ment he found equal confirmation of the inex-tricable embrace of time and timelessness and of the constancy of the bonds of humanity surviving both the precision of personality and the disruption of world conflict.

We should have lost the war from the outset if we had admitted that war was the whole of our lives and there was nothing else beyond it. Whereas the opposite is the case. Humanity is all our lives, and whoever wins this war, humanity—the decent average way of life—will prevail in the end, even over the victor.

For some also the point of the poems may lie in the fact that this belief in the value and beauty of life had withstood both the affirmation of war and the negative seeping of post-war cynicism—so that being subjected to both these experiences George Villiers could write without self-consciousness:

Spring to-day. The warmth of another season blushing through this February day and the thrushes and blackbirds forgetting the date and making strange fluting noises such as they make in April. . . . And when I came in my old nurse, who was staying with us, met me and began to chatter, starting every sentence with 'Do you remember that time?' Oh yes, I remember every time and somehow it all seems good to me, good to be alive, good to remember, even good just to Be.

M. V.

Contents

Dawn

THIS is the silver singing-team of the Dawn angels
High up among the wide graven clouds
Chanting of sunrise at the Gates of Day.
In order due bespread
Upon the puffed ridges,
And gyves of light and airy dawn-lit bridges,
Who so all-glorious as They?
Hear, how They pluck the glittering wires
Of their sickle-shaped and music-humming lyres
And, hand in hand,
Merge in wide silver flocks and thronging choirs,
To pour down over the silent world, still wrapt in dreams,
Grey mantled land and ever urgent sea,
Their harmony divided streams
Of dispassioned and boy-throated melody.

Blessed are the Moments

BLESSED are the moments when the spirit of man
    goes out to the spirit of Earth,
To merge and commingle therewith—
For here is Peace.

Blessed are the moments when man knows himself as
    the fairest flower of the Earth,
Thrown up by the Earth—
For here is Joy.

But blessed are the moments when he knows that
    the moving spirit of Beauty in all that he sees
Is the moving spirit of Beauty in the depths of his soul—
His own innermost soul—
For here is Truth at last; and Immortality at last;
And the ending of Doubt.

The Bowling Green

"To carve out dials quaintly, point by point,
Thereby to see the minutes how they run,
How many make the hour fall complete;
How many hours bring about the day;
How many——"

"Fred, try to put your wood between these two;
See my hand? That's jack-high.
These two are ours.
Try to put one here."

I look up from my corner in the shade:
The smooth, level spans of the lawn
Stretch away to the yews at the end;
The flowers at the foot of the yews
Hang their heads pitifully
In the hot sunshine.
It is very still—
Not a leaf stirs, not a sound,
Not a bird flutters in the heavy chestnuts above,
Or sings in the yews.
Only, far away in the valley somewhere
Smothered and faint,
A cuckoo calls once,
And a moment after,
The village clock strikes half past three.

The men stand at the jack-end of the rink
In the sun,
Coats off, hands on hips,
Or falling loosely at their sides,
Watching, waiting;
At their feet
The bowls lie clustered

Round the little white jack.
At the playing end,
Not three yards from where I sit,
A young lad stoops;
Bends one knee forward;
Straightens the other leg behind him
Presents the ball:
Plays. . . .

He is lithe and slim
With little clenched hips;
When he bends to play,
The muscles ripple along his back,
Half-seen beneath his shirt.
He is fair, with clear blue eyes
And golden hair and dusky skin,
An English lad.

The slow black ball sweeps cleanly over the grass:
Its cheeks seem to cling to the turf
Caressingly.
It lists with a wide gracious curve
Towards the goal at the end.
The players call and chaff,
As the wood comes into its rest
A foot from the jack.

" . . . How many days will finish up the year;
How many years a mortal man may live.
When this is known, then to divide the times.
So many hours must I tend my flock;
So many hours must I take my rest;
So many hours must I contemplate;
So many hours must I sport myself;"

"Try and come down the pitch to about here
Before you list——"

"So many minutes, hours, days, months, and years,
Passed over to the end they were created,
Would bring white hairs into a quiet grave."

"Yes, if you were to put a wood in here
Just kiss and touch him away and settle here yourself,
We'd win the end.
Could you do it, d'you think?
Try, allow plenty of land."

This game traditional!—This English scene!—

Ah, what does it matter,
What does it matter, I cry inwardly,
The separate life—
The pain—the fret—the heartache?
We *are* the things we love,
More than we know.
This peaceful afternoon, these silent trees,
This distant cuckoo-call,
This chiming clock,
This book upon my knee
Wherein all England lives,
This group of players on an English lawn—
These things are all the best of me!
And always they have been,
Always will be;
And always somehow, somewhere
(If love be aught)
I shall have part in them.

The Oxen

(Fragment)

LABOURED the wain, two sloping oxen bent
Slant-wise under the yoke, with stubbed and crooked knee,
Holding unhurried and majestic pace.

Patient beneath the collar they labour on,
Patient and slow, and in their eyes no pain.
Immediacy of thought, centered on need
Of action, or forebearance through their limbs.
As the great weight retarded is, or pushed,
Twin dewlaps ponderous sweep the ashen dust,
Before their cloven feet. The creaking cart,
Its rope lines set, its high blue collar
And its tasselled nets, drawn by the milk white pair;
Their marble faces carved like featured busts
Of calm dead Emperors and Statesmen gone. . . .

In February

"I AM the boyish savour in the wind, the breath
    and uprising of the flowers,
The young green milk in the sapling flowing,
The velvet on the——"

O heaven!—
As I walk home through the late winter dusk,
Making a song to the beat of my steps on the road,
The evening is full of the whisper of birds' wings
And their twitter and scuffle in the bushes;
And once a thrush
In the lace of an over-hanging bough
Gives that long low note
That April hears.

The heavens above me
Are like the gray dappled flank of a horse;
They move westward in a body
Quicker than I can go.
When I look up into the sky
I feel like a straw
Thrown on the surface of a racing stream,
Buffeted hither and thither,
Eddying—whirling—circling—
I stagger like a drunken man
When I look up.

I am the boyish savour of the wind, the breath and
    uprising of flowers,
The young green milk in the sapling flowing,
The velvet down on the leaf;
I dream in the far-away heavens,
The light on the edge of the cloud.

I skip with the black-legged lambs in the orchard,
For me, too, is the veined udder stretched,
The mother patient and standing.
I pull at the teat with my fellows,
The sweet milk comes in spurts,
And the warm infusion spreads over my body,
Giving me strength through my limbs.
I sing with the birds in the branches of the trees;
In a green gloom I sing the sorrowful cadences,
The love-plaint mingled with grief.
I am the hand that milks, the milk in the pail;
I am the springing of grasses and bursting of buds—
What though my spirit be locked in the loins of
     the hills—
Lo, I am the Spring!

A little air,
A little wanton air
Warm with the approach of flowers,
Whispers in the undergrowth
Or touches my cheek,
With sometimes such a meaning in it
As makes me stop, stock still,
And take deep breaths down in to the lower lungs,
Exulting, with rush of old memories
Released in the brain,
And sense of things far off,
And loveliness still to be sought for
And worshipped for ever
Through the years to come.

"I am the boyish savour of the wind, the breath and
     uprising of flowers
The velvet down on the——"
Hark!

As I turn in at the gate at the bottom of the garden,
That long, low note again.
The Thrush.
He is late.
He should be with the other birds
Somewhere in the fastness of the bushes,
With his soft brown head
Tucked under his wing,
Asleep.
Hark! Again—Again
And now no more.

O God, I cry, give me the song of the birds,
The need to sing each transient flash as it passes,
Happy or sad.
Roll back from my mind like clouds
The confusions and inhibitions of my mortality,
The spectres of Doubt and Fear, enthroned in the mind,
Obscuring the sense of Thy loveliness
As it comes to me ever;
Driving it under ground
To grope deep channels there, sightless and blind,
While Death keeps state above.
Let me slip the cerements of my mortal heritage
And mingle in essence with Thine onrushing Life,
Everlasting and divine,
Through birds and trees and rivers and flowers,
Through days and years;
Then shall I sing as this thrush
From the pressure of Beauty within
And Beauty without;
Then shall I sing as this thrush,
And my song will be true.

9

Winter

THE garden lies withered and frozen:
A thrush hops across the paved way
And disappears into the dry sticks
Of the flower-border:
He's looking for food.
Other birds come,
And I know there must be little rustling noises
In among leafless bushes.

Beyond—
The blur of the cold
Has eaten like acid into the heart of the landscape:
The breasts of the hills, the valleys and the coombs,
The tops of the trees in the middle distance—
All merge and mingle together
In a vast indistinguishable gloom;
And there is no courage anywhere,
Or hope anywhere—

But the little cottage-room is aglow in the firelight
There is warmth, and comfort, and peace;
And I sit at my writing-table,
A centre of human intelligence and divination,
With the whole universe in my head;
And in my heart
An inexpressible Wonder and Joy—
A Shining—a Splendour
As of God.

The Studio

THREE figures round a country fire
In a blue dusk sitting and talking,
The golden dapple of the flames
Chasing the smoky shadows to and fro
Over the cool white walls,
And over the dim frame of the great North window
Where still, high seen above the dark of the hill,
An orchard bough
Frets the troubled visage of the sleeping sky,
Fast fading into night . . .
Behind us
Vague shadowy furniture swimming in a semi-darkness,
Or smiling with long quiet gleams
Where the firelight touches it.
Somewhere a kettle singing.
A cat purring,
A clock ticking.

I sit with my cheek in my hand
Gazing into the hearth;
And in my mind a sudden vision from nowhere
Of golden mountains under a cobalt sky
Frowning down upon glinting white-roofed cities
Where the sour-faced camels go,
Threading their slow-foot way
Through bazaars
Burning with colour. . . .

Immortality

THE curve of the road in the dusk:
A moon overhead,
Gathering glory,
(I see my shadow behind me)—
Myself trudging home through the owlet light
Of the winter's eve.

Stubble-fields rounding the crest of the hill,
Wreathed in a little creeping mist—
The dying breath of the departing day
Made visible in the frore air,
Beautiful as a dream.

The beech copse—
Tall, sentinel trees,
Making a black lace against the sky,
Deathly still,
But speaking to me:
Saying a thing I understand:
Calling to me.

Over all—
Dominating all—
The hills,
Deepening divinely into the obliteration
Of the on-coming night.

O mystery! . . .

I am gone from myself—
I am every human being
Who has ever stood on a roadway, under a moon, at dusk,
With all the heaven of life in his heart,

And youth in his veins!
I am the moon, and the stars,
And the wind, and the rain,
And the blossom on the orchard bough in spring,
And the heart of a little child.
And I am the dog that barks in the valley,
And the partridge that calls in the meadow—

My spirit is the Spirit of Beauty and Love that moves
    in these things—
What though I die a thousand deaths,
Can It be destroyed?—

A great god-like laughter fills my chest;
And I walk home through the gathering dusk,
At peace with Life,
And with Death.

Spring, 1919

O ALL you weary over the whole world
Whose bitter grief is as a darkness furled
And cloud about your hearts. Whose lampless days
Must pass for ever widowed of those rays
Which gave them light to live; whose every breath
Is stricken and amazed at thought of Death
Coming to one so near, so loved, so known,
So one with you, so utterly your own,—
Whose frozen minds now stunned to nothingness
Reflect but one fact o'er, no more, no less,
One face, one form, one spirit like a star,
One life that burned constant, familiar,
One ample presence that fulfilled all Love
And what's beyond—one radiant heart above
The littleness and shallowness of Life,
Who held for you the balance twixt the strife,
'Twixt joy and pain, whose equalness is peace—
So that your spirit rode the quiet seas
In havened calm—how must you lift blind eyes
In wonder at the mocking skies
Grown jubilant again; and at the earth
Rejoicing in the million pleasured mirth
Of foaming life renewed!—How can you bear
To watch the sure revolving of the year
Sweeping you onwards, laughing as it goes
To blossom in the lily and the rose,
And deck the head now bowed in sightless gloom
With mocking flowers that dance about the tomb,
Yet know not of the dead. O you who mourn
And dare not look upon the springing corn
Lest its young blades be turned to barbed spears
Which find a pathway through your heart to pierce

Your grievous wounds afresh—we weep for you!
What service can we render? How renew
The widowed lives within these shrines of flesh
Now desolate? How capture and enmesh
Those spirits which like messengers are sped
To batter on the gateways of the dead
With unavailing hands of Love, when Fate
Must needs bid Love sink down disconsolate
Before its iron law? Oh, we who sing,
What solace can we give? What comfort bring
To ease you of the heartbreak of the Spring?

There is a Presence walks the changing year,
More lovely than the Delian wanderer
For all his golden youth, when in the groves
He strung his lyre and sang, and all the loves
Of earth and sea and sky gave trembling ear.
There is a Presence walks the changing year,
More swift than Dawn, more tremulous than Light,
Whose eager feet press close upon the flight
Of soft-winged days, that fly before it soon
(Like doves affrighted by a sudden swoon
That tells a mortal near) E'en so, E'en so
The Easter of our hopes is pressing near.

There is a Presence walks the changing year,
More beautiful than Life, more strange than Death,
More eager-hearted than the very breath
Of Love itself. It lives, It breathes, It speaks—
Its feet are on the ladder of the weeks,
Storming the fortress of old tyrant Time
Before the crocus springs, or the white rime
Is off the grass. The February birds
Do sing of Its approach; and gentle herds,

Low-lying on the land where keen winds blow,
Feel a faint stirring through the flock, and know
Its advent near. And we who know its ways,
Feel suddenly about our hearts the praise
Of elemental and stupendous things—
Dooms and decrees and splendours of dead Kings;
And blue seas breaking on to golden sands
Where coral blows; heroes, long since dead,
Who fought for Virtue with uplifted head
Against a world in arms; and fortune fair,
For all who have the heart to do and dare—
So mirroring Its substance on the earth
And in the hearts of men, It wakes to mirth
Perennially our laughter-loving race,
With urge divine of happiness and grace,
Giving uplifting strength for ventures new,
And Heaven's strong gift of love to see them through,
And peace to end them; while ever as It moves,
Across the abounding earth, Its spirit proves
The nothingness of Death. It bursts in green
Upon old forest oaks and elms serene,
Who smile in wonder at their tender shoots,
And nod their aged heads; while at their roots,
The self same living Spirit breathes and blooms
In trailing glory through fair golden glooms,
Where sweet birds hang divine and croon of love
In nestling solitude while far above,
It wanders in the diamond of the sky,
Touching the sullen clouds to ecstasy,
Till all the breathless heavens abase themselves
In dreamt youth again. It bursts on shelves
Of craggy rock, and shorn declivities
Where wild flowers cling, and tremble to the breeze
And know a world of space. It seeks the stream

And broods upon its surface, all a-dream
With hazy peace and even-flowing calm,
Shedding abroad that slow, delicious balm
That steals upon quiet lands where waters are.
Then at the river's edge, in many a star
Of creamy meadow sweet and celandine,
It congregates and bursts in flowery sheen,
Making an underworld of fond delight
And brilliant joy, melodious with the flight
Of reedy dragon flies, and fur-thighed bees;
It walks the meadows and the sloping leas,
Pouring its flood through golden-throated days,
Made lovely with the gentle song-birds praise
And all the busy noise of growing things
Unfolding secretly. It spreads soft wings
Protective round our farms, to ward off shocks,
So that the woolly mother of the flocks
May bear without amiss, and in the vales
Be tender bleatings when the young dawn pales,
Free from all fear of Nature's myriad dooms—
Then up It springs to play about old coombs
And cup-like dells, and other hidden places
That lie embosomed in the hills, to fill their mazes
With glaring leaf, and sudden light of flowers,
Where only yesterday the sodden hours
Had dropped the melancholy year away
In rayless gloom. It breathes through all decay,
And mocks at desolation and despair,
As if these twain, this nether hearted pair,
Were but the phantom nothings of man's brain:
Its negative assertion, without stain
Of valid victory, save only as the breath
And likeness of earth's own dim shadow Death,
Whose final empire cannot stand a day

17

Before God's own. And nought of earth can stay
The passage of that elemental fire,
In bud and leaf, as in the heart's desire
Of man himself. It gives the eternal hope:
The bursting of old bonds to give rich scope
To tidings new. The onward, upward rush,
The everlasting strength that naught can crush.
It is the fair in all things fair,
In man's own heart as in the vernal air;
It is the sheen upon the breast of birds:
It is the love and increase of the herds:
It is the wisest laws that man can teach:
It is that unknown something in a speech,
That wins a flowery pathway to the heart,
Engend'ring love,—aye and more: It is that part
And passion of a man that flames to deeds
When fear holds back: It is the winged steeds,
That bear Imagination to the brink
Of undreamed Heavens, where earthy senses shrink,
And Spirit dwells in naked hemispheres
Of Light and Love supreme, past hope and fears
And mortal wonderings; aye, more than this;
It is the very Godhead of all bliss,
Whose everlasting and pervading breath
Resolves the phantoms of our life and death
In one, cool clear, ineffable serene
Beyond the limits of things heard or seen,
Where we do find our human loves again,
Sans time, sans place, sans grip of the old pain
Mortality must breed; but ringed about
By a Divinity Who knows no doubt,
Whose reason is His Own sufficiency,
Against all thought,—the last necessity,
The Risen Christ, whose mirror is this Spring.

The Singer

(Fragment from *Ulysses*)

THROUGH the still night
He sang a known, a venerable song,
—A loved, a known, a venerable song—
Such as on the mellow days of summertime in Greece
The reapers used to chant, as with their scythes
They laid the bearded corn,
And bound and gathered it along the swathes,
Singing of Ceres and Earth's fruitfulness;
Or such as the good-wife told her little sleeping son,
What time she rocked the cradle with her foot,
While her two lovely hands
Fluttered like doves about the snow-soft wool,
Heaped in great piles about her quiet knees—
When the beech-logs blazed on the hearth-stone,
And the old dog slept,
And Tenderness prevailed, a living thing,
In the dim twilight, ere the men came home.

And as he sang,—
Comrades gathered round the watch-fires,
And heart expanded to heart, and speech arose,
Soft whispered speech of home, soft as the night. . . .

The Blackbird

WILL you remember me when the long days
    lengthen between us,
And there is no word, no look, no sign?—
When the days take to themselves days,
And the weeks weeks,
And the season changes, changes,
With the change in the leaf,
And the change in the tilth?
Will there be other laughter in your heart,
Other thoughts in your mind,
When the corn's gathered into the barns
And the team goes a-ploughing?—

And when you come in from the golden ways
    of the Autumn
To dream by a golden fire
At dusk,—
Will my image flicker awhile in your thoughts
Like the bickering flames?

Next Spring,
You will hear the blackbird waken in the thicket:
His song will come upon you suddenly,
Like a javelin,
Piercing your heart . . .
You will not have time to stop your ears,
Or put up your hand to your breast,
His song is too swift:

It will be upon you in a flash—
Through you in a flash—
Past you in a flash—
But, oh, the things it will leave in its wake,
The memories, the ecstasies! . . .

Will you remember me then?
Ah, Love, remember me then!

The Dun Cow

STABLED at Bethlehem assuredly, that dun cow,
Browsing in the distance with her wise English eyes;
The very same, may be, leaned over His manger-crib
And heard the English Angels on the roof
Sing "Hark the Herald" most composedly
As English angels should, or watched with curious eye
The simple shepherd's meek approach; Symbolic cow,
Assuredly, a Christmas cow,
Though summer is in the air.

The Motor Boat

OVER the wine-dark sea plashing and plunging—
Marvellously not collapsing or oversetting
In our little coracle of a motor-boat!—
The engine thrumming an accompaniment
To the crying and singing of the wind—
To the scream of the gulls—
To the buffet and fruther of foam,
When a wave catches our bows end-on,
And scatters the spray high over our heads,
As onward we plunge!

(White is our boat, like the dropped plume of a gull
In the trough of the wave,
And drenched with sunlight:
Amber and gold is our flesh in the gold of the sun,—
Our arms—and necks—and faces,—
Our hands.)

High over us
The bold and beautiful headlands
Lie long and lithe, projecting into the water,
Couchant, like drowsy leopards asleep in the sun.
We creep in round their jagged paws,
And look fearfully up
At their sleek flanks,—
Golden and ruddy they tower above us,
Adream in the haze of the sun,
And glistening with spray.

Great caps of green
Cling about their rugged brows,
Cropped and shorn by the wind
To a marvellous smoothness,—
Where the little wild thyme hides its head, I know,

And the sea-thrift clings,
Shrivelled and wild with the spray,
Trembling and nodding
Over vast abysses.
In places the wall of the granite is broken
And the land falls back in great answering rhythms and sweeps,

(Like the lilt of a song),
Beckoning, beckoning,—
Friendly with all manner of cultivation:
Rich with the chequer of fields,
And the falling together of woods:
Fair with farms, and the dwellings of men,
And the spires of churches—
Beckoning inland up narrow coombs and valleys
From little pebbly beaches
At the edge of the foam—
Beckoning ever inland from the waste of granite and sea.
Cornwall!—

We gaze up through the warmth and colour and
        splendour of it all:
In imagination we disembark on the narrow shelf of the beaches:
We adventure the coombs and valleys,—
Find little twisting pathways up from the sea,
Through oakwoods and coppices:
Past the low-lying gables of farms,
Emerging from elms—
Past rick-yards, dusty with chaff—
Through sloping orchards
Where the little streams gather and murmur,
On their way down the ravines
To the sea,—
Onward in spirit we go
Into the rich heart of the country,

Answering the beckoning, friendly call,—
The siren call of the land . . .
Then the implacable slope of the rock
Closes again,
And, quicker than thought,
We adjust our eyes to the grim smooth surfaces,—
The jagged edges,—
The wrinkles and furrows and crannies
Of the inevitable, inaccessible granite,
Where the gulls reel,
And the feet of the cliffs are awash
In the fret of the foam.
Seaward all is a dancing trouble
Of wine-dark water and spray,—
Illimitable spaces of it
Seeming forever and forever to be advancing upon us
In packed and tumultuous formation,—
Cavalry of the sea,
Line upon line surging up to us,
Breaking in upon us,
Enveloping us,—
Ridge upon ridge,—
Each with its crest of spray,
Its knot of the sweet white foam,
Laughing and gurgling,—
Slapping our prow,
As the gunwale rises and dips.
The vast dome of the air
Is drenched through and through with the sunlight:
Drunken with excess of the golden wine of it:
The far away heavens are cloudless and blue,
And sails are white on their breast.
(O dreams, dreams, wide-flung as the heavens themselves,
Rising from the inaccessible depths of consciousness

In answer to the illimitable spaces,—
The boundless freedom—the light,—the air,—
The splendour of sun and of wind,—
All restraint of convention and superstition
So marvellously dropping away,—
Dissolving like a wraith,—
Slipping backward into the eternity of things accomplished
    and done with:—
The spirit knowing its own,
Marvellously going out to it,
Stretching the consciousness to envelop it, and become one
    with it,—
Loveliness greeting loveliness
Within and without!)

Low over the foam flies a solitary gull
To join the white company of his fellows,
Gathered like dropped snow-flakes
On the broad sun-spaces of a smooth, low hummock of rock
At the foot of the cliffs.
He thrusts his white neck straight as he flies
To give a wild, strange, gabbling cry,
Piercing, insistent,—
Answered immediately in many-tongued, clamourous cacophony
From the group on the rocks.

The mackerel-trawlers are out:
In the distance we descry them,—
A colony of little black boats a-dream on the foam,
Their sleek dark flanks tossing and dipping
In the trough of the waves.
We pass three out together, hugging the shore,
Working a landward school.
We can see the brown arms of the men hauling and shifting,
Hear even their cries and laughter.

Our man at the tiller calls to them:
They call back with an answering shout.
Something passes between them,
(We know not what)
Some courtesy of the sea,
Some greeting . . .
Their shouts die away upon the water,
As onward we plunge!

(O dreams, dreams, wide-flung as the heavens themselves,
Rising from the inaccessible depths of consciousness
In answer to the illimitable spaces,—
The boundless freedom,—the light,—the air,—
The splendour of sun and of wind—
All restraint of convention and superstition
So marvellously dropping away,—
Dissolving like a wraith,—
Slipping backward into the eternity of things accomplished
    and done with,—
The spirit knowing its own
Marvellously going out to it,
Stretching the consciousness to envelop it, and become one
    with it,—
Loveliness greeting loveliness,
Within and without!)

Polperro!—
Already we have arrived in the little harbour,
And the roar of the sea
Is left far behind.
This quiet is like waking
From a turbulent dream
To find the hush of the morning upon you:
We are amazed at it;

And our cheeks are still aglow with the wind,
Here, where no wind is.
We creep in under the high protecting rock;
And houses appear,
Clambering up the precipitous slopes
On both sides,
And in the middle,—
Tier upon tier—
Little friendly-faced houses with jagged roofs,
Tumbling one upon another
In talkative, comfortable confusion,—
Scrambling for a place
In the narrow circle of the little cove.
The gulls wheel and cry round the jetty
And the nets are out to dry,—
Festoons of them hung on the sea-wall,
Gleaming browns and umbers, and ochres, and blacks,
Against the grey of the stones. . . .

Three lounging men,
With incurious eyes,
Watch us approach.
They smoke placidly in the sun,
And do not speak. . . .
An open space of pavement, glistening wet,
The fish market!—
(We are almost alongside now.)
The barrels stand packed in a row—
 The barrels and boxes, ready for the London market—
And there are great scales in the corner for weighing.
(The stench of stale fish is all pervading and overpowering;
But the houses, the little friendly houses
Smile down a welcome,
Happy and quiet in the sun,

As we approach.)
We disembark, running up the wet steps,
Laughing, with the spirit of adventure.
I carry the cushions and the tea-basket,
And other paraphernalia
Of a picnic.
Laden, we set forth.
Where shall we go?
All is a new world to us, thrilling and strange.
We feel the weird new sense of it,
Clamouring at the gates of consciousness,
Seeking to be known, installed in our minds, loved.

The little houses call to us:
"Come and discover us:
We are quiet and happy here, with the sun and the sea:
We are old in men's love,
And know the secrets of life:
The generations are born in us,
And go forth from us,
And come back to us:
There is much love in us,
And memory in us;
And we are full of quaint, creaking furniture,
And chattering clocks.
Come and discover us!"—

Through the little hushed streets, narrow and silent,
We thread our adventuring way,
Silent ourselves,
For fear of disturbing something.—
(We know not what; but there's something we mustn't disturb—
A feeling, a Presence . . .)
Up and down steps we go—
Round twisting corners—

Under archways—
Down little whispering gullies of streets
That lead to the sea.
And ever the houses speak to us, deliver their message to us,—
Their message of those who toil in the sea,
And return from the sea to love, to sleep, to die.
Year after year,
Generation after generation,
It is always the same . . .
We look in at the open doors.
There are little mats on the floor,
And china ornaments packed on the mantel-piece;
No-one's about.
But we have caught the message;
We know—we understand—we are there—
The heart of the place is kind and familiar:
We are accepted . . .

How many hours—how many hours
Do we spend discovering and investigating?
How many hours on the rocks, sitting and talking and dreaming,
Lulled by the song of the tide,
The whisper and lisp of it
Fretting the feet of the cliffs
Aeons below?—
At last we turn homeward again.
(Is it all Eternity we have spent there?
Are we two souls descending out of heaven,
From the detached and incurious life of the worlds above,
Into the clamour of earth?
Ah, who shall say?)

Homeward again!—
Over the wine-dark sea plashing and plunging—

Marvellously not collapsing or oversetting
In our little coracle of a motor-boat!—
The engine thrumming an accompaniment
To the crying and singing of the wind—
To the scream of the gulls—
To the buffet and fruther of foam,
When a wave catches our bows end-on,
And scatters the spray high over heads,
As onward we plunge!—
Homeward again—
The purple evening deepening divinely
Round us and about us,—
The heavens alive and on fire in the West:
The zenith glimmering with the opalescence of dusk,—
Night coming up from the sea.

(O dreams, dreams, wide-flung as the heavens themselves,
Rising from the inaccessible depths of consciousness,
In answer to the illimitable spaces,—
The boundless freedom,—the light,—the air,—
The splendour of sun and of wind,—
All restraint of convention and superstition
So marvellously dropping away,—
Dissolving like a wreath,—
Slipping backward into the eternity of things accomplished and
    done with;
The spirit knowing its own,
Marvellously going out to it,
Stretching the consciousness to envelop it, and become one
    with it,—
Loveliness greeting loveliness
Within and without!)

Heaven

Great tales they tell of Heaven's Court,
  Of Thrones and Powers and Kings:
Of jasper walks and Gates of Pearl
  And such-like stately things.

But I have seen on Heaven's Green
  The English geese go wrangling,
And spied in green, celestial lanes
  The English inn-signs dangling.

"The Chequers" and "The Golden Lion"
  I've view'd in Heaven's Shire
With rubbed gold letters along their fronts
  Of Somebody's "Entire."

And an old rough pony out to grass
  By the dusty roadside edge
With tall, still nettles growing out of the ditch
  And a haystack over the hedge . . .

I know not if it's blasphemous
  To deem such things must be;
But without such homely things in Heaven
  'Twould not be Heaven for me!

Values

WHAT does it matter
If I cannot express myself as I wish?—
If I am poor and companionless,
And have a half-uttered love in my heart,
And a pain in my mind,
And in all my senses,
Because of it?—
What does it matter
If my contemporaries shun me,
And think me mad?—
If I ride the middle-heavens of life, like a lonely star
Which has swung from the orbit of its constellation
Into an edgeless void?—
What does it matter
If I'm lost,
Or damned,
Or dead,—

If *still* the everlasting glory of God
Be poured out over all the lands of the earth,
In streams of inextinguishable Beauty—
If still the flowers laugh in the happy sunshine,
And the warm spring grasses wave in the wind,
And the lambs run to their mothers in the orchard
Under the blossom—
If still there be courage in the hearts of men,
And love in the hearts of women,
And Life, coming and going upon the Earth,
Bringing Freedom and Joy?

Nocturne

(Two on a Terrace)

A GREY uniformity of tone
Passes its hand over the eyes of the dusk,
Obliterating all detail,
All definition.
Sea and sky faint together,
And are mingled and lost
In a vast meaningless stare,
Gleaming and wan.
Only the giant brows of the headland
Above and beyond us
Stand out in colossal relief,
Hullish and beast-like,—
A great block of tone,—
A tremendous profile,—
Shimmering black against the eye of the sea.

A grey uniformity of tone
Covers all consciousness,
Invades it,
Masters it ever more wholly and completely,
As the minutes slip on into night.
The soul seems caught up and enshrined in it,
Evoking a mood marvellous with the texture of it,—
Opalescent, with strange quiet gleams, deep and prophetic,
Speech issuing therefrom, hushed and subdued,
But ever deeper going
Into the profound tranquillities
Which lie at the root of life,—
Sentences, like dull red flames—flickering—
Falling—dying—flickering again,—
Twixt spirit and spirit.

34

In Gloucestershire

THERE is a valley where the Spring comes soon
And lingers late afield, till even June
Must woo the lazy blossom from the trees;
An inland vale, hill circled, where the breeze
Whispers and roams, or wanders haltingly
About the embosomed fields, or, springing free,
Makes a diviner, sharper minstrelsy
Above the upland pastures: where the pines
Gesture and sway in dark, close-huddled lines;
A land of spacious calm, where bellied clouds
Build castles in the sky, or billowy shrouds
To feature the April heavens with intent,
Till man's imagination may invent
A thousand thousand phantasies to vie
Within his mind—and people the great sky
With creatures of his choice, his mood to charm;
A land of ease, where a manorial farm,
Deep in the law of England's lovely prime,
Mothers the country's sure increase; where time
Hangs heavy on the wheel, the more to woo
A contemplative quiet; where ring doves coo
In hidden glades; and in belated coombs,
The leaf deepens divinely on the looms
Of the advancing Spring; and sorrows cease
On green-lit lawns, beneath the sky's deep peace;
A land of sloping orchards, to line the streams
That gather and murmur through lush fields where dreams
Lie furled about the everlasting hills,
Whose every lovely shape and seeming fills
Some vacant space within the heart
With praise of the Undying—

Here thro' many days,

35

Towards the unseen Spirit in things seen
That hides its splendour in this lap of green,
It is my joy so to direct my course
That sometimes I may woo it in my verse
In dancing lyrics and enraptured words,
Which fly across my brain as swift as birds
Its powers and its perfectness to prove.
Nor have I lack of fellowship and love!
For there are men who dream and pray and sing
And go upon their ways unhurrying—
Where all is hurry in the world without—
For sight here, with wisdom girt about,
Whose vision, being fixed beyond the days and hours,
Perceives Eternity in little flowers
And love in speechless things. These are my friends,
And when the happiness of the long day ends
By some congenial board, or golden fire,
When all is hushed that could the senses tire
I sit with them and have thrice blessed speech;
Open and frank; familiar, each to each,
Until the hour grows late, or my heart longs
To muse divinely on the birth of songs,
And so I take my leave. . . . Some men may scoff,
Yet what is left to fill their lives enough
When the false gods they worshipped and adored
Sink down into the gloom, with never a word,
And all is one—the losses and the gains?
The Spirit lives, and only that remains.
In its high honour is it so small a thing
To dream a little, and a little sing?

Reflections on a River Bank

ORDER we how we may in this high world,
Twisting the image of ourselves to fit the case,
With many buffettings worn to a patina
Our rugged edges, till that which meets the eye
Not we ourselves but the smooth thing the world has made.
Here where the image of a stream translucent is,
Reflecting the white nothing of the sky:
Here on this verdurous, soft rustling bank
Where nothing stirs save the adventurous breeze
Gingerly fingering the spears of the tall bull-rushes;
Companied with the near plop of the trout for music:
Here after the nefarious gloom of cities,
Bespeak we ourselves to the innocent air,
Whose Holiness is for the having;
  White whimpled clouds, ridged like sand in the aboveness,
What pure gesture do you bring to furrowed and contracted
    brows,
To the pale forehead and to the restless heart,
From your dreaming aloofness.
Do you collate strange vastness in ourselves, subliminal heights,
With your flocculent ridges and wise depths?
You are the patience of the Kingdom.
And now along the levels see the white nakedness of life
Crave intricacy and involvement: be secret in the grass
And hide up its innocence in the white cups of flowers
And close stubble grass. O here is fugue enough
With variations enough upon a never ending theme;
Music enough for a mind to prelude with.
This is the high summer—
Dancing time of the green meadows,
Gold and white with the splashed foam of flowers
And knee-deep cattle in the pasture. June,

Highstepping summer pause before the drowsy latter time,
The summer-golden sleepy August time,
With creaking carts of the stuffed golden grain
And heavy dusty leafage in the going. More lovely June! . . .
Fast flyer in the clear, wind speckled cloud
Hazed only in the sweet pensive sense of you,
And dear dazed going in the fields and lanes.
Is there a place in the heart where all these things, ever
Linked from year to year with many a happy event
And many a secret sorrow, yet lives a maturity
Summered to perfection in a world of tears.
Loveliness garnered and guarded.
High summer-mood, June levels,
Wheeling together of the white secret thing in us
As in the Other. O, angel guarded, Ineffable,
Win me to the high mood of you this day,
Here where your peace droops to me through the
    minstrel-stream,
Singing in the meadow to the sunsmitten air
And frolic shadow on the grass. I know too well
How thought's inveteracy would cut you into qualities:
Fling adverbs and epithets and the thundering verb
About your path to catch and capture you—
And put you in a cage with golden bars,
As man may parrots. But I am wiser far.
My most irrational song, associative only,
Is so soft as your bright wing may brush against
Unscathed. Stay. I will not capture you.

Sometimes in Self-Forgetfulness

SOMETIMES in Self-Forgetfulness
Adream on the broad gold day,
I feel the breath of a greater song
   Than yet I can convey.

But distantly, oh, distantly—
Brushing the edge of sense;
And indistinct, like thunder, heard
   Many valleys hence.

If troublous men go o'er the earth
And cleave the restless sea
Contesting Earth's golden fruits
   What is this to me,

If I can hear the meadow grass,
And every flower and bird
Proclaim some hidden syllable
   Of the Eternal word.

Lord, wake in me this gift of song
And I'll not count amiss
The lack of all men hanker for
   Of gold, or fame, or bliss.

Thy patient eremites of song
Spent all their tireless youth
Serving, through long lapse of years,
   The unhurried ways of Truth.

They stood intent to watch and wait,
Not cut off from their kind,
But finding in the midst of things
   A stillness of the mind.

Grant that in self forgetfulness
Myself, as still as they,
May feel the breath of a greater song
   Coming to me some day.

Day-Dreams

WE are gathering apples in the orchard,
Up on the hill
By Washbrook Farm.

The men are there
With their bill-hooks, and ladders, and baskets,
And there's a great to-do,
With voices crying and calling,
And laughter
Under the trees. . . .

(Oh the men
Looking up in the boughs,
And shading their eyes with their hands,
Their arms and necks and faces a-gleam in the sunlight,
Dusky and gold!)

There's a stirring and shaking
In the leaves overhead;
And the tops of the trees
Dance in the sunlight,
Backwards and forwards,
Against the blue;
And the fruit patters down to the ground
With a little whispering rush
Through the trellis of leaves.

The children come out
With their mother and the white-frocked nurses.
They sit, spread out upon the grass,
Like flowers. . . .

My little son runs laughing towards me,—
Clutching the coat of a shaggy old dog that he loves.
He takes my hand and looks up at me;—
And the blue of his eyes
Is the blue of all the seas I have known;
And the gold of his hair
Is the gold of all the dawns I have worshipped;
And a great spasm of joy
Leaps through my being. . . .

(O, the games we have by the up-turned cart,
The running from tree to tree!—
The laughter and frolic and fun!—
The thrills and adventures!)

Evening comes,
And the ruddy October day,
With its burden of red-gold woods
And patient skies,
Sinks down into the bosom of the dusk;
And the dusk rises up to meet it,
Like a drowsy lover awakening
Out of the valley below. . . .

Now the shadows prevail in the orchard,
And colour has flown,
And a crescent moon, like the slipper of a god,
Is gathering strength overhead,
Tipping the dew-drenched spears of the grass
With its ghostly gleam—
And we pass into the firelight,—
The comfort, and welcome and peace
Of the old, grey, whispering house,
The house which is Home.

Prayer

LORD GOD of the oak and the elm,
And of the grey-green fields,
And the silver skies;
Lord God of the birds and the clouds,
And the rustling of leaves—

Ah, Green Bough in my heart burgeoning, blossoming,
All the days of my youth have been spent in the courts
    of Thy praise!
I have loved Thee, worshipped Thee, adored Thee;
I have uncovered my heart where Thou liest hid,
That men might behold thine infinite healing and mercy;
Thou hast been my Refuge and Strength.
Be with me still,
When my life creeps into the shadows;
When Age has consumed my Endeavour,
And Ardour has flown:
When the hills are dreamy with April,
And I scarce can see them for dimness;
When the children laugh and call in the lane,
And I cannot go out to them . . .
Be with me still;
Shake down thy dusky dew over the fading landscape
    of my day;
And when the darkness comes,
Set Thou thy stars and constellations
In the heavens of my peace,
That still, through the watches of the night,
I may behold Thee, worship Thee, adore Thee—
And in the Great Dawn
Can praise Thee,
O Lord my God, my Lover, and my Friend.